I0814001

An Imprint of Pop!
popbooksonline.com

World Religions

HINDUISM

by Elizabeth Andrews

This book is filled with videos, puzzles, games, and more! Scan the QR codes* while you read, or visit the website below to make this book pop.

popbooksonline.com/hinduism

abdobooks.com

Published by Pop!, a division of ABDO, PO Box 398166, Minneapolis, Minnesota 55439.

Printed in China.

052023
082023

Cover Photo: Shutterstock Images

Interior Photos: Shutterstock Images, Getty Images, Himalayan Academy Publications, Kapaa, Kauai, Hawaii

Editor: Tyler Gieseke

Series Designer: Laura Graphenteen

Library of Congress Control Number: 2022950555

Publisher's Cataloging-in-Publication Data

Names: Andrews, Elizabeth, author.

Title: Hinduism / by Elizabeth Andrews

Description: Minneapolis, Minnesota : Pop!, 2024 | Series: World religions | Includes online resources and index

Identifiers: ISBN 9781098244453 (lib. bdg.) | ISBN 9781098245153 (ebook)

Subjects: LCSH: Hinduism--Doctrines--Juvenile literature. | Hinduism--Customs and practices--Juvenile literature. | World religions--Juvenile literature. | Religious belief--Juvenile literature.

Classification: DDC 294.5--dc23

*Scanning QR codes requires a web-enabled smart device with a QR code reader app and a camera.

TABLE OF CONTENTS

CHAPTER 1

BRAHMAN AND SACRED TEXTS

People follow different religions across the world. A religion is an organized practice of faith and **worship**. Hinduism is the oldest major religion. It dates back more than 3,000 years.

Hindu holy texts are written in the ancient language of Vedic Sanskrit.

Hinduism is practiced all over the world but started in India. All Hindus practice in their own ways. There is no set of specific beliefs to follow. Instead, each person worships different forms of the Brahman.

Statues of Brahman have three faces to represent the three main forms of the god.

Brahman is a **divine** being that is the **universe** and everything inside of it. All Hindu gods and goddesses are forms of Brahman. The spirit of Brahman lives in all Hindus. Gods and goddesses have important, individual roles. By worshipping them, a Hindu worships Brahman.

Brahman breaks down into three main gods. Brahma is the creator god, Vishnu is the **preserver** god, and Shiva is the destroyer. Hindus believe that the universe is made, destroyed, and remade in a 4.3-million-year cycle. All three forms of Brahman play a role in this cycle.

The guidelines for Hinduism come from **sacred** texts. The Four Vedas are the basis of Hindu religion. The Vedas give guidance on how to worship the Hindu **deities**. Other religious writings include the Upanishads, which help followers understand the Vedas.

The Puranas cover everything from yoga, proper army organization, and the caste system to the gods and goddesses. The *Bhagavad Gita* is a book

The *Ramayana* and *Mahabharata* are major epic poems that cover the tales of Hindu gods and heroes and their struggles.

that explains that all people face hard decisions, but they must make choices according to their dharma.

POPULAR HINDU DEITIES

CHAPTER 2

DHARMA AND SAMSARA

Dharma are the **moral** laws that guide a Hindu and their duties to the world. When Hinduism began, all people were divided into groups. The organization is called a caste system. The top caste is the Brahmains. They are religious leaders. Below them are warriors and rulers called

LEARN MORE HERE!

Kshatriyas. The third caste, Vaishyas, are the commoners. At the bottom are the Shudras, who are laborers.

Marigold flowers are often used in Hindu practices. They represent the sun and positivity.

The Rig Veda says the caste system was created from the body of **divine** being. This story teaches that the roles of each caste have a religious purpose.

The wheel of samsara shows the six realms a soul can be reborn into.

The Dalit class is the lowest social level. People from this class are not treated well and must work in very unpleasant conditions.

Every caste's purpose keeps the world in balance. Hindus believe karma and samsara decide a person's position in the caste system.

Samsara is the cycle of birth, death, and rebirth. A person's soul in Hinduism is **eternal**. It does not die when the body dies. Instead, the soul goes into another body and lives another life. The new bodies can be plant, animal, or human. The new body is decided by the karma in the soul's previous lives.

The eternal soul of a person is called the *atman*.

Karma describes action. It can be good or bad. The more good deeds a person does, the better the karma. And with good enough karma, the person will be reborn higher in the caste system. Hopefully, a Hindu lives a life without hurting another living thing. If people do a lot of bad, they might be reborn as insects!

Breaking free from samsara is called moksha. It is a Hindu's greatest purpose. To reach moksha, a Hindu must understand the oneness of the **universe**. Brahman is the universe. And a soul's true nature is to reconnect with Brahman.

Kindness creates good karma. The person who did the nice action might experience something nice done for them soon after.

CHAPTER 3

REACHING MOKSHA

Hindus take different paths to be released from samsara. However, all paths usually include practicing **rituals** and performing one's duties. Hindus also study the soul and Brahman. They devote themselves to a certain god or goddess.

EXPLORE LINKS HERE!

Some Hindus wear a small dot called a bindi on their foreheads.

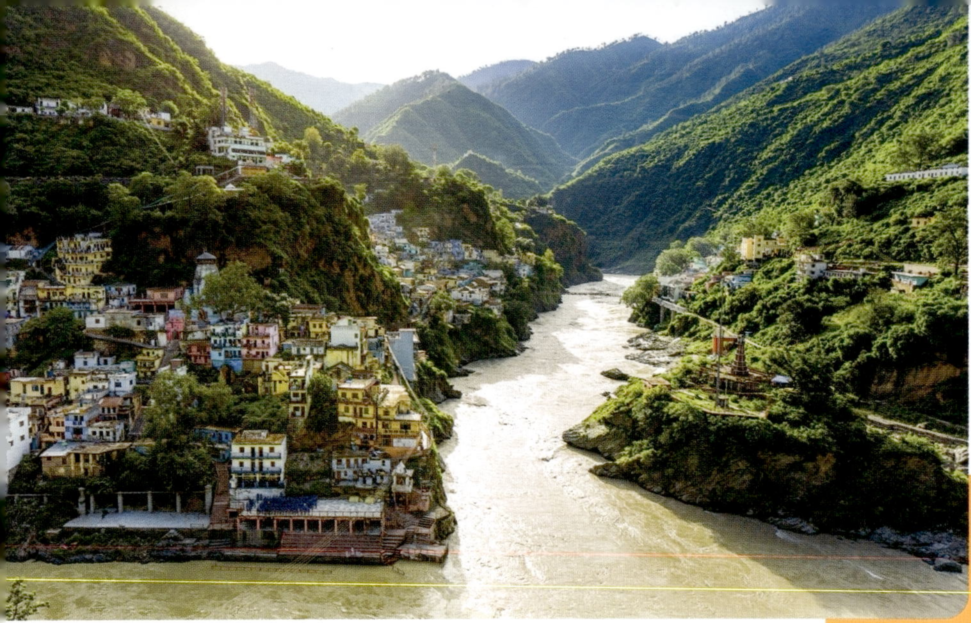

The Ganges River is wide and slow moving.

Different Hindus **worship** different gods and goddesses. They pray to images of their **deities** at home or at a temple. They offer gifts such as fruit,

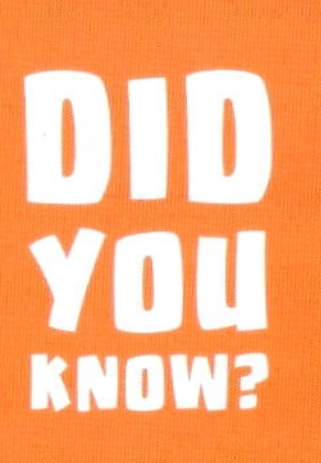

DID YOU KNOW?

The Ganges River is the most important river for Hindus. It physically represents the goddess of purification and forgiveness, Ganga.

perfumes, and flowers. They bathe the images and **chant**. The chants come from the Vedas or other texts. Hindus call these rituals *puja*.

Hindus value nature. They believe it is physical evidence of the **divine** on Earth. Many rituals take place in rivers and mountains. Usually, the rituals are for cleansing the mind, body, and soul of sin. There are teachers and leaders called gurus who help Hindus through their pujas with the goal of moksha.

GHANDI

Mahatma Gandhi was a Hindu leader. He helped free the people of India from British rule using nonviolent tactics. Though he was Hindu, Ghandi was most concerned with people living peacefully together no matter their religion.

Another religious practice that Hindus perform is yoga. Yoga connects a Hindu with the divine. It brings together the

Hindus may meditate by focusing on the thoughts and feelings that go through their minds.

Yoga can strengthen a person's body and help with physical and mental balance.

mind, body, and soul to reach oneness with Brahman. People can learn yoga from gurus called yogis.

Meditation pairs with yoga. It quiets the mind. Meditation helps Hindus let go of chasing wisdoms, passions, and even goodness. Those can stand in the way of reaching moksha.

CHAPTER 4

COLORFUL CELEBRATIONS

There are many Hindu festivals for gods and goddesses. The celebrations might include music and food. They may also include pujas and meditations. The festivals often focus on a specific **deity** or **sacred** natural feature.

COMPLETE AN ACTIVITY HERE!

Holi is a day that celebrates love. People play in streets and parks. They throw colorful powder called gulal at each other.

Hindus may create rangoli *art on the floor near the entrance to their homes.*

Hindus wear colorful, traditional clothing to celebrate Diwali.

Diwali is a famous festival of lights that represent good defeating evil. It's a five-day celebration where people decorate their homes and temples with oil lamps and string lights. Hindus clean their homes and wear new clothes. They do this so everything is nice when they invite the goddess Lakshmi into their homes. She is the goddess of prosperity.

Another popular Hindu holiday is Holi. It celebrates and welcomes the coming of spring. People spray each other with colored powders. Each color has a meaning. Yellow represents the

Just like spring flowers bloom and burst with color, so does the Holi festival!

god Vishnu who made clothing out of sun rays. Red is for love, green for new life, and blue for the god Krishna. It's a very fun and joyful celebration.

People take trips to holy sites such as the Ganges River looking for purification.

There are also important puja and events for each Hindu throughout their life. Mothers stay home during pregnancy to avoid evil. There are naming ceremonies for young children. Weddings are big events in the Hindu community. There will be days of celebrations with food and pujas.

Hinduism is full of color, thrilling stories, and exciting gods and goddesses. Millions of people practice it all over the world in their own way. It is an important world religion that will continue to change over time.

Oil lamps lit during Diwali are called ***diyas.***

MAKING CONNECTIONS

TEXT-TO-SELF

What part of Hinduism are you most curious about? Please explain your answer.

TEXT-TO-TEXT

Have you read any books about different religions? How were those religions similar to or different from Hinduism?

TEXT-TO-WORLD

Hinduism is one of the longest-lasting world religions. Why do you think it has stood the test of time compared to other religions with deities like Greek and Roman mythology?

GLOSSARY

chant — words spoken in rhythm over and over.

deity — a god or goddess.

divine — having to do with gods or goddesses.

eternal — lasting forever.

moral — ideas and patterns of behavior that relate to what is right and what is wrong.

preserver — a being who keeps something in its original state or condition.

ritual — a set of actions always done in the same way, often because of tradition.

sacred — having to do with religion.

tactic — a plan used to achieve a goal.

universe — all existing things including the Earth and heavens.

worship — love, respect, and affection shown to an object, person, or being.

INDEX

DiscoverRoo!
ONLINE RESOURCES

This book is filled with videos, puzzles, games, and more! Scan the QR codes* while you read, or visit the website below to make this book pop.

popbooksonline.com/hinduism

*Scanning QR codes requires a web-enabled smart device with a QR code reader app and a camera.